SIMPLY DIET FOR BEGINNER VEGETARIANS

Top 50 Fresh And Delicious, Easy And Quick Keto Recipes On A Budget To Help You Start Vegetarian Ketogenic Diet Lifestyle!

EMILY LEWIS

TEXT COPYRIGHT © [EMILY LEWIS]

TABLE OF CONTENT

Chapter One:
Overview of the Ketogenic Diet for Beginners

Introduction

The ketogenic diet is based on utilizing carbs as an energy source which uses fats as the main energy source for the working of the body. The keto vegetarian diet comprises on specifically plant-based foods which are rich in carbs and can be used as the main energy source for the effective and healthy working of the body. The diet has numerous health benefits which include enhanced efficiency of the body, healthy metabolism, and the most important one i.e. weight loss. This book is going to cover every aspect regarding the keto vegetarian diet and the entire process of ketosis for better understanding of beginners for following this diet plan. Thus, a wide range of options for nutritious, yet delicious recipes on the cheap will also be introduced to vegetarians who are about to embark on ketogenic diet.

What does "keto" means?

The body starts using ketones instead of glucose as an energy medium for its working after shifting on a ketogenic diet. The ketones are responsible or the word 'keto' in the diet plan are utilized in the minimum presence of blood sugar in the body. Ketones are produced by eating a low carb diet and a mild protein supply. The main production source of ketones are fats and they are produced in the liver. They are used for the working of the body including the brain.

Alteration to ketones from glucose results in excessive fat burning while lowering insulin levels in the body. This has a very impulsive effect on losing weight apart from various other health benefits. The effective method to achieve ketones i.e. production of ketones is to fast. But as fasting can't be done for a longer time, keto diet is an alternative approach to fasting, having the same benefits like fasting but without actually fasting at all.

Who Shouldn't Go for the Ketogenic Diet?

In general cases the keto diet is perfect but people with falling under the following categories are to consult their doctors before going on this diet, these include:

- Diabetic Patients
- Blood Pressure related Patients
- Breastfeeding Mothers

Advice for Breastfeeding Mothers and Diabetics:

It is very dangerous to eat a strict low-carb diet while **breastfeeding**, a safer low-carb diet would be having 50g carbs/day. You can achieve this by adding 3-4 large fruits to your strict plan, in case of any abnormality or complication, immediately visit a doctor. It is also advised to drink an adequate supply of water to lower the risk of dehydration for better milk production. Enhance your fiber, fats and veggie intake for maintaining your energy levels. For breastfeeding, it is preferred to consider a slightly moderate keto plan instead of a strict one.

At first, it's not recommended for **diabetics** to go for the keto diet, in case you want to be on the diet plan, strictly check your blood sugar levels on daily basis to keep them under the normal levels. You also have to keep a check on ketone levels in your body to avoid the risk of DKA (Diabetic Ketoacidosis) or in rare cases coma. It is recommended by the ADA (American Diabetes Association) to test your ketones if your blood sugar surpasses 240 mg/dL. It is also advisable for those with type 2 diabetes to stick to the ketogenic diet as a phase, not as long-term treatment of the disease.

Chapter Two:
Advantages of Keto Diet

The advantages of keto diet are almost similar to other diets based on low carb intake; the only difference is that the keto diet is more powerful and efficient in its benefits. In simpler words, the keto diet is a low carb diet plan with super-charged powers compared to its competitors and has maximum benefits to offer for the users. A few of its major benefits are as follows:

Weight Loss:

The fact that the body uses fats as an energy source logically explain how the keto diet is beneficial in weight loss. Fat loss is stimulated as the insulin levels are dropped low. This situation provides an ideal situation for drastic fat loss, resulting in weight loss effectively without hunger. It is to note that, above 20 modern types of research has verified that the keto diet is more effective than other similar diet plans in its weight loss factor.

Controlled Appetite:

The keto diet lets you control your appetite. This is due to the fact that, when fats are burned drastically, the body has access to surplus energy from them and results in a reduction of hunger.

This control of appetite also results in more effective weight loss. It also eases the intermittent fasting, stimulates the reversal of type-2 diabetes apart from stimulating weight loss. It is also very feasible financially as it reduces your expenditure on food due to less hunger.

The lower urge to eat food or controlled appetite also helps a lot to avoid sugar and food addiction alongside eating disorders like bulimia etc. The feeling of satisfaction is an integral part of the solution. Food becomes a friend and a fueling source instead of an enemy with the ketogenic diet plan.

Surplus Energy and Mental Boosting:

The process of ketosis provides a steady flow of energy in the form of ketones to the brain resulting in avoiding blood sugar swings. This results in improvement in mental focus and concentration and also clear away brain fog too. The main reason for the popularity of the keto diet is tits benefits regarding mental health and focus. These benefits can be easily experienced while being in ketosis. During ketosis, the human brain is provided with surplus energy round the clock in the form of ketones instead of carbs which is the reason for the improved mental performance of the human body.

Reversing Type-2 Diabetes & Controlling Blood Sugar:

Although ketogenic diet is not scientifically acknowledged as a long-term solution to type 2 diabetes, it is credited to the fact that keto diet lowers down blood sugar levels in the body and also lowers the negative role of higher insulin levels. The fact that keto diet is very efficient in reversing type-2 diabetes also suggests that it is very helpful in avoiding it in the first place apart from reversing pre-diabetic conditions.

Improvement in Health Markers:

Lower carb intake results in improvement in critical health markers like blood sugar levels, cholesterol levels (triglycerides and HDL) and in blood pressure. These health markers are associated with metabolic syndrome, weight improvements, reversal of type-2 diabetes and waist circumference etc.

Stomach Improvement:

Keto diet has many efficiency improvements in stomach health. It lowers cramps and pains alongside less or entirely no gas at all in the stomach. It can be experienced within the initial 2-3 days of following the ketogenic diet plan. FODMAP contains a high amount of carbs and they start fermentation in the small intestine which leads to bloating and gas. The gut walls are unable to absorb them properly and cause the fluid stuck in the intestine thus resulting in diarrhea. The keto diet is a much low

FODMAP diet and acts as an anti-IBS approach. The slow removal of carbs from your diet improves your digestive system befittingly.

Improvement in Physical Strength:

Ketogenic diet improves physical strength and endurance a lot due to the provision of a regular and constant supply of energy from fats. Energy due to carbs (glycogen) in the body only for a few hours of high-level exercising, contrary to this the energy from fat sources lasts for weeks or even months in the body and enhances the physical performances of the body.

Epilepsy Treatment:

The keto diet is very beneficial for the treatment of epilepsy since the 1920s. In the initial days it was used for children only but now it has also been applied to adults and has shown improvements in them. With ketogenic diet, patients of epilepsy either take less or even not a single medication for their treatment without the fear of any seizures. This also lowers the side effects of drugs by lowering drug intake and plays a role in mental health improvement.

The most beneficial thing about the keto diet is that it lets epilepsy patients stop taking much lower medications for the disease and yet able to control epilepsy. In some cases, they can even get rid of this medication without having the risk of any seizures. Anti-epilepsy drugs have side effects like concentration loss, drowsiness etc. which can be evaded with the keto diet by getting rid of the medications.

Additional Benefits:

Apart from the above-mentioned advantages, there are certain benefits which are life-changing for certain people. The lower intake of carbs has many advantages like migraine control, lesser acne issues, blood pressure controlling and even aids in certain mental health complications. A few additional benefits of the ketogenic diet are listed as below:

- Lesser Acne

- Reversing PCOS (Polycystic Ovary Syndrome)

- Fever Heartburn

- Fewer Migraine Attacks

- Treatment of Brain Cancer

- Lesser Sugar Cravings

- Curing Alzheimer

- BP level controlling

Chapter Three:
How to achieve 'Ketosis'?

Many factors play a critical role in improving and increasing the ketosis levels. They are listed below in the order of their importance from high to low:

Restriction of carbs

Reducing carb intake to just digestible 20grams/day or lower which is a strictly low carb diet can improve the ketosis levels a lot. It is important to understand that fiber intake doesn't have to be lowered as it is a beneficial nutrient. It is important to note that solely lowering carb consumption can result in ketosis and the rest of every measure taken for ketosis improvement ensures the success of ketosis.

Restriction of Proteins

Restricting the protein intake to moderate levels is very important in the ketogenic diet plan. Surplus consumption of proteins will result in their conversion into glucose and thus lowering the ketosis levels. The most commonly committed mistake by keto followers is higher consumption of proteins which should be reduced to moderate consumption only. The ideal amount of protein intake should be 1g/kg the weight of the body i.e. approximately 80g of protein if you are 80kgs.

Consume Enough Fat:

There is a difference between fasting and keto diet for ketosis. The ketogenic diet plan can be followed in a constant manner while continuous fasting is impossible to achieve rather harmful to the body. The negative impacts of starving involve hunger, tiredness and giving up while the ketogenic diet can be easily applied to daily lives and followed without any hurdle with a lot of benefits. Eating enough fat is important and if you are feeling hungrier all the time, try adding a bit more fat to your meals like more olive oil etc.

Try Avoiding snacking:

It is recommended to avoid snacks when you're not hungry. Eating above your needs has drastic effects on ketosis and it slows the process of ketosis alongside slowing weight loss too. You can opt for a ketogenic snack in case of unavoidable hunger.

Intermittent Fasting

Instead of complete fasting, intermittent fasting aids a lot in ketosis. The most effective intermittent fasting is eating only for 8 hours in a day and fasting during the rest of the 16 hours. It is very effective in raising ketone levels, reversal of type-2 diabetes and stimulating weight loss.

Regular Exercising

Exercising alongside lower carb consumption moderately stimulates the process of ketosis. In addition to this, it also improves weight loss process and reversal of type-2 diabetes in a light manner. Exercising is not essential to achieve ketosis rather it assists in improving ketosis.

Sufficient Sleep

The standard of having enough sleep is considered at an average of 7-8 hours per night. It is recommended to get sufficient sleep time and keep your stress levels lower. Stress hormones and sleep deprivation result in raising blood sugar levels, lowering ketosis levels and slightly effects in slowing down weight loss too. It also makes it hard to follow the keto diet plan and avoid temptations for eating contrary to the plan. Sound sleep and lower stress level don't lead into ketosis rather aids in improving the process.

Conclusively, to achieve ketosis, lower the carb intake to extremely low levels. It is preferred to lower them to approximately 20 carbs/day. IT is the most essential factor for the occurrence and achieving of ketosis. For improving ketosis levels, start adopting the above-mentioned factors from top to bottom.

No Need for Additional Products

It is not necessary to go for expensive and high priced fancy supplements like ketone supplements or MCT oil. There is no scientific or medical evidence to prove that these supplements are beneficial in weight loss or disease reversing at all. Ketone supplements are not beneficial in lowering blood sugar levels or insulin levels and they certainly aren't helpful in fat burning too. They are slightly beneficial in weight loss or reversal of type-2 diabetes. These supplements are sold on a commission basis for salesmen and people are made to fall for their high prices without them having any scientific evidence for the effectiveness of these products.

These products might be beneficial in improving physical and mental performances for a very short time span. They also are beneficial slightly in raising blood sugar levels which only last for a few hours, comparing their high prices, these products are of no use at all. Instead of them strictly follow your keto diet plan for effective benefits the plan offers.

Note: How to Avoid Lacking Nutrition

The keto diet means cutting off a lot of foods from your diet which is considerably high on carb content. This might lead to certain minerals and vitamin deficiencies and result in complications like keto insomnia, keto rash, and keto flu etc. These problems can be avoided by considerable planning and awareness to maintain your mineral and vitamins content as required by your body.

1. Loss of Vitamins: Following steps should be taken for overcoming the deficiencies of the respective vitamins:

    - Vitamin D: To overcome Vitamin D deficiency, get adequate dairy and go out in the daytime for absorbing sunlight.

    - Vitamin B Complex: To avoid its deficiency, simply get enough leafy green veggies and foods rich in proteins. These foods include dairy products and nuts etc.

    - Vitamin K: Vitamin K can be enhanced by taking dark leafy green veggies like kale, broccoli, and spinach etc.

2. Loss of Minerals:

    Unwanted conditions like the keto flu etc. which are resulted due to a sudden reduction in carb content can be avoided by having an adequate supply of various minerals. These include:

3. Calcium:

Calcium deficiency can be overcome by consuming broccoli, Bok choy, kale and dairy products etc.

4. Potassium:

Potassium loss is the most commonly deficient nutrient on the keto diet. Its deficiency can lead to constipation, muscle cramps and weakness etc. Potassium can be taken in an ample amount in the form of spinach, kale, avocado, and mushrooms.

5. Magnesium:

Magnesium is the 4th mineral which is found in abundance in our bodies. Its deficiency will result in fatigue, muscle cramps, and dizziness etc. You can enhance your magnesium intake by taking nuts, cacao powder, spinach, and dark chocolate.

6. Sodium:

Sodium content gets lowered more abruptly in the form of sweating while being on the keto diet. It can be taken in an adequate manner by consuming 1000-2000 mg sodium/day.

Chapter Four:
Foods for Keto Vegetarian Diet
Foods which are recommended

Grasping the right foods to eat is crucial to a ketogenic diet success. The following foods are considered to be the most effective for the keto vegetarian diet plan. They are 'keto-friendly' as being low in carbohydrates and high in nutrients.

Not all kinds of vegetables are able to comply with ketogenic diet rules as some of them are high in carbohydrates and sugar. **Above ground veggies** like cauliflower, broccoli, cucumber, zucchini etc. can be eaten without worry. You can also stick with **leafy green veggies** like kale and spinach etc.

As a general rule of thumb, you have to be very careful with the amount of sugar you may consume from fruits. Low-sugar fruits such as **cherries, oranges, apples, plums, berries** like blackberries, raspberries and other impact berries, are low glycemic in nature and thus, will be a wise choice for your diet plan. Rich in healthy fats, full of vitamins and nutrients, yet super low in carbs, **avocados** are definitely a perfect fit for ketogenic diet.

Fermented foods have been shown to be naturally good for your immune and digestive system, especially while on a high-fat diet and therefore they should be incorporated regularly into ketogenic meals. You will want to look for products in fermented forms such as sauerkraut, kimchi, fermented ginger, sugar-free yogurt, kefir or amasai, grass-fed cheese, beet kvass, natural pickles, fermented assorted veggies.

The following foods are also ideal for your ketogenic diet:

- Seeds and nuts like almonds, pumpkin seeds, sunflower seeds, and pistachios etc.

- Sweeteners like monk fruit, erythritol, stevia and other sweeteners which are low carb in nature.

- Vegan 'meats' like seitan, tempeh & another vegan 'meats' which are low-carb & high-protein.

Foods which are not recommended

The following categories of foods are not allowed while following the keto vegetarian diet plan. These foods are high in their carb content and can have a negative effect on your plan:

- Legumes like peas, lentils, and black beans etc.

- Grains like cereals, rice, wheat, and corn etc.

- Sugar-rich foods like maple syrup, agave, and honey etc.

- Tubers like yams and potatoes etc.

- Fruits like oranges, bananas, and apples etc.

Protein Carb Ratio

Your food on the keto vegetarian plan should be mainly high in fat content and mildly high in protein as protein is convertible in the body to body sugar. A rough sketch suggests that approximately 5% energy should be from carbs (lower the number of carbs, the more the effectiveness). 15-25% should be from protein and almost 75% should be from fat.

How to Consume More Fat?

The main source of fats in the keto diet is high-fat dairy and eggs. They are many additional fat sources too which can be utilized on the keto diet. These include various plant-based oils which can be used as an alternative to the animal fats generally used for baking and cooking purposes. Some of these fat sources are as follows:

- Coconut Oil

- MCT Oil

- Avocado Oil

- Olive Oil

- Red Palm Oil

There are many other plant-based oils too, which can be used as a fat source but the above mentioned are versatile and healthiest.

What is recommended for Drinking?

Water is considered to be the most recommended and perfect beverage for keto lovers. In addition to water, coffee and tea can also be consumed but it is to be kept in mind that you shouldn't use any sweeteners, sugar in specific. A little quantity of milk or cream in coffee or tea is acceptable but not a coffee latte. The occasional consumption of a single glass of wine is also allowed.

Recipes for Keto Vegetarians:

Breakfast Recipes

1. Strawberry Milkshake

Serves: 2

Preparation Time: 10 minutes

Ingredients:

1 cup fresh strawberries

2 tablespoons Erythritol

1 tablespoon almonds, chopped

1 cups unsweetened almond milk

½ cup heavy whipping cream

½ teaspoon organic vanilla extract

¼ cup ice cubes

Instructions:

In a high-speed blender, add all ingredients and pulse until smooth.

Transfer into 2 serving glasses and serve immediately.

Nutrition Information per Serving:

Calories: 167

Fat: 14.6g

Carbohydrates: 8.1g

Protein: 2.2g

2. Green Smoothie

Serves: 2

Preparation Time: 10 minutes

Ingredients:

2 cups romaine lettuce, chopped

1 cup fresh baby spinach

1 cup fresh baby kale, tough ribs removed

¼ cup fresh mint leaves

2 tablespoons fresh lemon juice

8-10 drops liquid stevia

1½ cups filtered water

½ cup ice cubes

Instructions:

In a high-speed blender, add all ingredients and pulse until smooth.

Transfer into 2 serving glasses and serve immediately.

Nutrition Information per Serving:

Calories: 36

Fat: 0.4g

Carbohydrates: 7g

Protein: 2.2g

3. Smoothie Bowl

Serves: 3

Preparation Time: 15 minutes

Ingredients:

2 cups frozen strawberries

½ cup unsweetened almond milk

¼ cup fat-free plain Greek yogurt

1 tablespoon unsweetened whey protein powder

3 tablespoons fresh strawberries. Hulled and sliced

Instructions:

In a blender, add frozen strawberries and pulse for about 1 minute.

Add almond milk, yogurt, and protein powder and pulse until desired consistency is achieved.

Transfer the mixture into 2 serving bowls evenly.

Serve with the topping of walnuts.

Nutrition Information per Serving:

Calories: 87

Fat: 1.4g

Carbohydrates: 9.8g

Protein: 10.2g

4. Overnight Porridge

Serves: 2

Preparation Time: 10 minutes

Ingredients:

2/3 cup full-fat coconut milk

½ cup hemp hearts

1 tablespoon chia seeds

½ teaspoon organic vanilla extract

4 drops liquid stevia

Pinch of salt

2 tablespoons fresh raspberries

Instructions:

In a large glass jar, add all ingredients except raspberries and stir to combine well.

Cover the jar and refrigerate overnight.

Divide into 2 serving bowls evenly.

Top with raspberries and serve.

Nutrition Information per Serving:

Calories: 271

Fat: 21.2g

Carbohydrates: 8.1g

Protein: 13.7g

5. Blueberry Pancakes

Serves: 3

Preparation Time: 15 minutes

Cooking Time: 21 minutes

Ingredients:

½ cup almond flour

2 tablespoons coconut flour

½ teaspoon organic baking powder

1 teaspoon ground cinnamon

1½ tablespoon Erythritol

¼ cup unsweetened almond milk

3 large organic eggs

¼ cup fresh blueberries

Instructions:

In a high-speed blender, add all ingredients pulse until a thick mixture is formed.

Transfer the mixture into a large bowl and gently, fold in blueberries.

Set aside for about 5-10 minutes.

Heat a lightly greased skillet over medium-low heat.

Add about ¼ cup of the mixture in skillet and with the back of a spatula, spread the mixture into desired thickness.

Immediately, cover the skillet and cook for about 4 minutes.

Uncover and carefully, flip the side.

Cook for about 3 minutes or until golden brown.

Repeat with the remaining mixture.

Serve warm.

Nutrition Information per Serving:

Calories: 231

Fat: 16g

Carbohydrates: 12g

Protein: 11.8g

6. Simple Crepes

Serves: 2

Preparation Time: 15 minutes

Cooking Time: 12 minutes

Ingredients:

2 tablespoons coconut oil, melted and divided

2 organic eggs

1 teaspoon Splenda

1/8 teaspoon sea salt

2 tablespoons coconut flour

1/3 cup heavy cream

Instructions:

In a bowl, add 1 tablespoon of oil, eggs, Splenda, and salt and beat until well combined.

Slowly, add flour, beating continuously until well combined.

Add heavy cream and stir until well combined.

Grease a large non-stick skillet with remaining oil.

Add ¼ of the mixture and tilt the pan to spread into a thin layer.

Cook for about 3 minutes, flipping once after 2 minutes.

Repeat with the remaining mixture.

Nutrition Information per Serving:

Calories: 319

Fat: 27.4g

Carbohydrates: 10.9g

Protein: 8g

7. Cheese Waffles

Serves: 8

Preparation Time: 15 minutes

Cooking Time: 48 minutes

Ingredients:

1 cup golden flax seeds meal

1 cup almond flour

¼ cup unflavored whey protein powder

2 teaspoons baking powder

Salt and freshly ground black pepper, to taste

1½ cups cheddar cheese, shredded

¾ cup unsweetened almond milk

¼ cup unsalted butter, melted

4 large organic eggs, beaten

Instructions:

Preheat the waffle iron and then grease it.

In a large bowl, add flax seeds meal, flour, protein powder, and baking powder and mix well.

Stir in cheddar cheese.

In another bowl, add remaining ingredients and beat until well combined.

Add egg mixture into the bowl with flax seeds meal mixture and mix until well combined.

Place the desired amount of the mixture into preheated waffle iron.

Cook for about 4-6 minutes or until golden brown.

Repeat with the remaining mixture.

Serve warm.

Nutrition Information per Serving:

Calories: 383

Fat: 31.2g

Carbohydrates: 9g

Protein: 17g

8. Lemon Muffins

Serves: 6

Preparation Time: 15 minutes

Cooking Time: 20 minutes

Ingredients:

¾ cup blanched almond flour

¼ cup golden flax meal

1/3 cup Erythritol

2 tablespoons poppy seeds

1 teaspoon baking powder

3 large organic eggs

¼ cup heavy cream

¼ cup salted butter, melted

3 tablespoons fresh lemon juice

1 teaspoon organic vanilla extract

20-25 drops liquid stevia

2 teaspoons fresh lemon zest, grated finely

Instructions:

Preheat the oven to 350 degrees F. Line 12 cups of a muffin tin with paper liner.

In a large bowl, add the flour, flax meal, poppy seeds, Erythritol, and baking powder and mix well.

In another bowl, add eggs, heavy cream and butter and beat until well combined.

Add egg mixture into flour mixture and mix until well combined and smooth.

Add lemon juice, organic vanilla extract, and liquid stevia and mix until well combined.

Gently, fold in lemon zest.

Transfer the mixture into prepared muffin cups evenly.

Bake for about 18-20 minutes or until a toothpick inserted in the center comes out clean.

Remove the muffin tin from oven and keep on a wire rack to cool for about 10 minutes.

Carefully invert the muffins onto a wire rack to cool completely before serving.

Nutrition Information per Serving:

Calories: 250

Fat: 22.6g

Carbohydrates: 7g

Protein: 8.5g

9. Pumpkin Bread

Serves: 24

Preparation Time: 20 minutes

Cooking Time: 1 hour

Ingredients:

1 2/3 cups almond flour

1½ teaspoons organic baking powder

½ teaspoon pumpkin pie spice

½ teaspoon ground cinnamon

½ teaspoon ground cloves

½ teaspoon salt

8-ounces cream cheese softened

6 organic eggs, divided

1 tablespoon coconut flour

1 cup powdered Erythritol, divided

1 teaspoon stevia extract powder, divided

1 teaspoon lemon extract

1 cup homemade pumpkin puree

½ cup coconut oil, melted

Instructions:

Preheat the oven to 325 degrees F. Lightly, grease 2 loaf pans.

In a bowl, mix together almond flour, baking powder, spices, and salt.

In a second bowl, add cream cheese, 1 egg, coconut flour, ¼ cup of Erythritol and ¼ teaspoon stevia and beat until smooth.

In a third bowl, add the pumpkin puree, oil, 5 eggs, ¾ cup of Erythritol and ¾ teaspoon of stevia and beat until well combined.

Add the pumpkin mixture into the bowl of flour mixture and mix until just combined.

Place about ¼ of pumpkin mixture into each loaf pan evenly.

Top with cream cheese mixture in each pan evenly, followed by the remaining pumpkin mixture.

Bake for about 50-60 minutes or until a toothpick inserted in the center comes out clean.

Remove the bread pans from oven and keep onto wire racks to cool for about 10 minutes.

Carefully invert the bread onto a wire rack to cool completely before serving.

With a sharp knife, cut the bread loaves in desired sized slices and serve.

Nutrition Information per Serving:

Calories: 141

Fat: 12.7g

Carbohydrates: 3.7g

Protein: 3.9g

10. Spinach Omelet

Serves: 2

Preparation Time: 15 minutes

Cooking Time: 6½ minutes

Ingredients:

4 large organic eggs

¼ cup cooked spinach, squeezed

2 scallions, chopped

2 tablespoons fresh parsley, chopped

½ cup feta cheese, crumbled

Freshly ground black pepper, to taste

2 teaspoons olive oil

Instructions:

Preheat the broiler of oven. Arrange a rack about 4-inches from heating element.

In a bowl, crack the eggs and beat well.

Add remaining ingredients except for oil and stir to combine.

In an ovenproof skillet, heat oil over medium heat.

Add egg mixture and tilt the skillet to spread the mixture evenly.

Immediately, reduce the heat to medium-low and cook for about 3-4 minutes or until golden brown.

Now, transfer the skillet under broiler and broil for about 1½-2½ minutes.

Cut the omelet into desired size wedges and serve.

Nutrition Information per Serving:

Calories: 289

Fat: 22.7g

Carbohydrates: 3.8g

Protein: 18.4g

Entrée Recipes

11. Fresh Veggie Salad

Serves: 8   Preparation Time: 20 minutes

For Dressing:

5 tablespoons olive oil

3 tablespoons fresh lemon juice

2 tablespoons fresh mint leaves, chopped finely

1 teaspoon Erythritol

Salt and freshly ground black pepper, to taste

For Salad:

2 cups cucumbers, peeled and sliced

2 cups tomatoes, sliced

1 cup black olives

6 cups lettuce

1 cup mozzarella cheese, cubed

Instructions:

For dressing: in a bowl, add all ingredients and beat until well combined.

Cover and refrigerate to chill for about 1 hour.

For the salad: in a large serving bowl, add all ingredients and mix.

Pour dressing over salad and toss to coat well.

Serve immediately.

Nutrition Information per Serving:

Calories: 124

Fat: 11.4g

Carbohydrates: 5.4g

Protein: 2g

12. Strawberry Salad

Serves: 4

Preparation Time: 15 minutes

Ingredients:

6 cups fresh baby greens

2 cups fresh strawberries, hulled and sliced

1 tablespoon fresh mint leaves

¼ cup olive oil

2 tablespoons fresh lemon juice

¼ teaspoon liquid stevia

1/8 teaspoon paprika

1/8 teaspoon garlic powder

Salt, to taste

Instructions:

For the salad: in a large serving bowl, add greens, strawberries, and mint and mix.

For dressing: in a bowl, add remaining ingredients and beat until well combined.

Pour dressing over salad and toss to coat well.

Serve immediately.

Nutrition Information per Serving:

Calories: 141

Fat: 14.7g

Carbohydrates: 1.8g

Protein: 2g

13. Pumpkin Soup

Serves: 4

Preparation Time: 15 minutes

Cooking Time: 20 minutes

Ingredients:

2 teaspoons coconut oil

1 small yellow onion, chopped

½ teaspoon fresh ginger

2 tablespoons fresh cilantro, chopped

3 cups pumpkin, peeled and cubed

1 garlic clove, chopped

4 cups vegetable broth

Salt and freshly ground black pepper, to taste

½ cup heavy cream

2 tablespoons fresh lime juice

1 teaspoon pumpkin seeds

Instructions:

In a large soup pan, heat oil over medium heat and sauté onion, ginger, and cilantro for about 2-3 minutes.

Add pumpkin, garlic, and broth and bring to a boil

Reduce the heat to low and simmer, covered for about 15 minutes.

Stir in salt and black pepper and remove from heat.

In a blender, add soup mixture with cream and lemon juice in batches and pulse until smooth.

Garnish with pumpkin seeds and serve immediately.

Nutritional Information per Serving:

Calories: 111

Fat: 8.3g

Carbohydrates: 9.1g

Protein: 1.6g

14. Broccoli Soup

Serves: 4

Preparation Time: 15 minutes

Cooking Time: 15 minutes

Ingredients:

4 cups low-sodium vegetable broth

20-ounces small broccoli florets

12-ounces cheddar cheese, cubed

Salt and freshly ground black pepper, to taste

1 cup heavy cream

Instructions:

In a large soup pan, add broth and broccoli over medium-high heat and bring to a boil.

Reduce the heat to low and simmer, covered for about 5-7 minutes.

Stir in cheese and simmer for about 2-3 minutes, stirring continuously.

Remove from heat and with an immersion blender, blend the soup until pureed.

Return the pan over medium-low heat.

Stir in salt, black pepper, and cream and simmer for about 2 minutes.

Serve hot.

Nutritional Information per Serving:

Calories: 340

Fat: 26.5g

Carbohydrates: 8.2g

Protein: 18.5g

15. Veggie Stew

Serves: 4

Preparation Time: 15 minutes

Cooking Time: 21 minutes

Ingredients:

2 tablespoons olive oil

1 yellow onion, chopped

2 teaspoons fresh ginger, grated

1 teaspoon ground turmeric

1 teaspoon ground cumin

Salt and freshly ground black pepper, to taste

1-2 cups water, divided

1 cup cabbage, shredded

1 cup broccoli, chopped

2 large carrots, peeled and sliced

Instructions:

In a large soup pan, heat oil over medium heat and sauté onion for about 5 minutes.

Stir in ginger and spices and sauté for about 1 minute.

Add 1 cup of water and bring to a boil.

Reduce the heat to medium-low and simmer for about 10 minutes.

Add vegetables and enough water that covers the half of vegetable mixture and stir to combine.

Increase the heat to medium-high and bring to a boil.

Reduce the heat to medium-low and simmer, covered for about 10-15 minutes, stirring occasionally.

Serve hot.

Nutritional Information per Serving:

Calories: 109

Fat: 7.4g

Carbohydrates: 10. 8g

Protein: 1.8g

16. Stir Fried Veggies

Serves: 6

Preparation Time: 15 minutes

Cooking Time: 10 minutes

Ingredients:

2 tablespoons butter

1 pound frozen okra, thawed, trimmed and sliced

½ of green bell pepper, seeded and chopped

2 celery stalks, chopped

1 small yellow onion, chopped

2 cups tomatoes, chopped finely

Salt and freshly ground black pepper, to taste

Instructions:

In a large non-stick skillet, melt butter over medium heat and sauté okra, bell pepper, celery, and onion for about 5-6 minutes.

Stir in tomatoes, salt, and black pepper and cook for about 3-4 minutes.

Serve hot.

Nutritional Information per Serving:

Calories: 84

Fat: 4.1g

Carbohydrates: 10g

Protein: 2.3g

17. Creamy Brussels Sprout

Serves: 5

Preparation Time: 15 minutes

Cooking Time: 20 minutes

Ingredients:

1½ pound fresh Brussels sprouts, trimmed and halved

3 garlic cloves, minced

2 tablespoons butter, melted

2 tablespoons Dijon mustard

½ cup heavy whipping cream

Salt and freshly ground white pepper, to taste

Instructions:

Preheat the oven to 450 degrees F.

In a large roasting pan, add Brussels sprouts, garlic and butter and toss to coat well.

Roast for about 10-15 minutes, tossing occasionally.

Meanwhile, in a small pan, add remaining ingredients over medium-low heat and bring to a gentle boil.

Cook for about 1-2 minutes, stirring continuously.

Serve Brussels sprouts with the topping of creamy sauce.

Nutritional Information per Serving:

Calories: 148

Fat: 9.8g

Carbohydrates: 13.6g

Protein: 5.3g

18. Cauliflower Casserole

Serves: 4

Preparation Time: 15 minutes

Cooking Time: 35 minutes

Ingredients:

1 large head cauliflower, cut into florets

2 tablespoons butter

2-ounces cream cheese softened

1¼ cups sharp cheddar cheese, shredded and divided

1 cup heavy cream

Salt and freshly ground black pepper, to taste

¼ cup scallion, chopped and divided

Instructions:

Preheat the oven to 350 degrees F.

In a large pan of boiling water, add cauliflower florets and cook for about 2 minutes.

Drain cauliflower and keep aside.

For cheese sauce: in a medium pan, add butter over medium-low heat and cook until just melted.

Add cream cheese, 1 cup of cheddar cheese, heavy cream, salt, and black pepper and cook until melted and smooth, stirring continuously.

Remove from heat and keep aside to cool slightly.

In a baking dish, place cauliflower florets, cheese sauce, and 3 tablespoons of scallion and stir to combine well.

Sprinkle with remaining cheddar cheese and scallion.

Bake for about 30 minutes.

Serve hot.

Nutritional Information per Serving:

Calories: 243

Fat: 22.4g

Carbohydrates: 3.8g

Protein: 8g

19. Spinach Pie

Serves: 5

Preparation Time: 15 minutes

Cooking Time: 38 minutes

Ingredients:

2 tablespoons butter, divided

2 tablespoons onion, chopped

1 (16-ounce) bag frozen chopped spinach, thawed and squeezed

1½ cups heavy cream

3 organic eggs

½ teaspoon ground nutmeg

Salt and freshly ground black pepper, to taste

½ cup Swiss cheese, shredded

Instructions:

Preheat the oven to 375 degrees F. Grease a 9-inch baking dish.

In a large skillet, melt 1 tablespoon of butter over medium-high heat and sauté onion for about 4-5 minutes.

Add spinach and cook for about 2-3 minutes or until all the liquid is absorbed.

In a bowl add cream, eggs, nutmeg, salt, and black pepper and beat until well combined.

Transfer the spinach mixture in the bottom of prepared baking dish evenly.

Place the egg mixture over spinach mixture evenly and sprinkle with cheese.

Top with remaining butter in the shape of dots at many places.

Bake for about 25-30 minutes or until top becomes golden brown.

Serve warm.

Nutritional Information per Serving:

Calories: 599

Fat: 59.5g

Carbohydrates: 8.2g

Protein: 11.6g

20. Stuffed Zucchini

Serves: 4

Preparation Time: 20 minutes

Cooking Time: 18 minutes

Ingredients:

4 medium zucchinis, halved lengthwise

1 cup red bell pepper, seeded and minced

½ cup Kalamata olives, pitted and minced

½ cup tomatoes, minced

1 teaspoon garlic, minced

1 tablespoon dried oregano, crushed

¼ teaspoon red pepper flakes, crushed

Salt and freshly ground black pepper, to taste

¼ cup feta cheese, crumbled

¼ cup fresh parsley, chopped finely

Instructions:

Preheat the oven to 350 degrees F. Grease a large baking sheet.

With a melon baller, scoop out the flesh of each zucchini half. Discard the flesh.

In a bowl, mix together bell pepper, olives, tomato, garlic, oregano, red pepper flakes, salt, and black pepper.

Stuff each zucchini half with veggie mixture evenly.

Arrange zucchini halves onto the prepared baking sheet and bake for about 15 minutes.

Now, set oven to broiler on high.

Top each zucchini half with feta cheese and broil for about 3 minutes.

Garnish with parsley and serve hot.

Nutritional Information per Serving:

Calories: 95

Fat: 4.4g

Carbohydrates: 12g

Protein: 4.6g

Snack Recipes

21. Roasted Almonds

Serves: 16

Preparation Time: 5 minutes

Cooking Time: 10 minutes

Ingredients:

2 cups whole almonds

1 tablespoon chili powder

½ teaspoon ground cinnamon

½ teaspoon ground cumin

½ teaspoon ground coriander

Salt and freshly ground black pepper, to taste

1 tablespoon olive oil

Instructions:

Preheat the oven to 350 degrees F. Line a baking dish with a parchment paper.

In a bowl, add all ingredients and toss to coat well.

Transfer the almond mixture into the prepared baking dish in a single layer.

Roast for about 10 minutes, flipping twice in a middle way.

Remove from oven and keep aside to cool completely before serving.

You can preserve these roasted almonds in an airtight jar.

Nutritional Information per Serving:

Calories: 78

Fat: 6.9g

Carbohydrates: 2.9g

Protein: 2.6g

22. Cheese Biscuits

Serves: 8

Preparation Time: 15 minutes

Cooking Time: 15 minutes

Ingredients:

1/3 cup coconut flour, sifted

¼ teaspoon baking powder

Salt, to taste

4 organic eggs

¼ cup butter, melted and cooled

1 cup cheddar cheese, shredded

Instructions:

Preheat the oven to 400 degrees F. Line a large cookie sheet with a greased piece of foil.

In a large bowl, mix together flour, baking powder, garlic powder, and salt.

In another bowl, add eggs and butter and beat well.

Add egg mixture into flour mixture and beat until well combined. Fold in cheese.

With a tablespoon, place the mixture onto prepared cookie sheets in a single layer.

Bake for about 15 minutes or until top becomes golden brown.

Nutritional Information per Serving:

Calories: 142

Fat: 12.7g

Carbohydrates: 0.8g

Protein: 8g

23. Baked Veggie Balls

Serves: 8

Preparation Time: 15 minutes

Cooking Time: 25 minutes

Ingredients:

2 medium sweet potatoes, peeled and cubed into ½-inch size

2 tablespoons unsweetened coconut milk

1 cup fresh kale leaves, trimmed and chopped

½ small yellow onion, chopped finely

1 teaspoon ground cumin

½ teaspoon granulated garlic

¼ teaspoon ground turmeric

Salt and freshly ground black pepper, to taste

¼ cup ground flax seeds

Instructions:

Preheat the oven to 400 degrees F. Line a baking sheet with parchment paper.

In a pan of water, arrange a steamer basket.

Place the sweet potato in a steamer basket and steam for about 10-15 minutes.

In a large bowl, place the sweet potato and coconut milk and mash well.

Add remaining ingredients except for flax seeds and mix until well combined.

Make about 1½-2-inch balls from the mixture.

Arrange the balls onto the prepared baking sheet in a single layer and sprinkle with flax seeds.

Bake for about 20-25 minutes.

Nutritional Information per Serving:

Calories: 61

Fat: 2.1g

Carbohydrates: 9g

Protein: 1.5g

24. Celery Crackers

Serves: 15

Preparation Time: 15 minutes

Cooking Time: 2 hours

Ingredients:

10 celery stalks

1 teaspoon fresh rosemary leaves

1 teaspoon fresh thyme leaves

2 tablespoons raw apple cider vinegar

¼ cup avocado oil

Salt, to taste

3 cups flax seeds. Grounded roughly

Instructions:

Preheat the oven to 225 degrees F. Line 2 large baking sheets with parchment paper.

In a food processor, add all ingredients except flax seeds and pulse until a puree forms.

Add flax seeds and pulse until well combined.

Transfer the dough into a bowl and keep aside for about 2-3 minutes.

Divide the dough into 2 portions.

Place 1 portion in each prepared baking sheets evenly.

With the back of a spatula, smooth and press the dough to ¼-inch thickness.

With a knife, score the squares in the dough.

Bake for about 2 hours, flipping once halfway through.

Remove from the oven and keep aside to cool on the baking sheet for about 15 minutes.

Nutritional Information per Serving:

Calories: 126

Fat: 7.6g

Carbohydrates: 7.1g

Protein: 4.3g

25. Deviled Eggs

Serves: 12

Preparation Time: 10 minutes

Ingredients:

12 hard-boiled large organic eggs, peeled and sliced in half

½ cup mayonnaise

½ teaspoon salt

Cayenne pepper, to taste

Instructions:

With a spoon, scoop out the egg yolks from each egg half and transfer into a large bowl.

With a fork, mash egg yolks slightly.

Add mayonnaise and salt and mix well.

Scoop the mayonnaise mixture in the egg halves evenly.

Serve with the sprinkling of cayenne pepper.

Nutritional Information per Serving:

Calories: 101

Fat: 7.6g

Carbohydrates: 2.7g

Protein: 5.6g

26. Avocado Guacamole

Serves: 4

Preparation Time: 10 minutes

Ingredients:

2 small ripe avocados, peeled, pitted and chopped

½ cup fresh cilantro leaves, chopped finely

1 tablespoon fresh lime juice

Pinch of freshly ground black pepper

Instructions:

In a bowl, add all ingredients and with a fork, mash until well combined.
Serve immediately.

Nutrition Information per Serving:

Calories: 145

Fat: 13.8g

Carbohydrates: 6.2g

Protein: 1.4g

27. Sweet Potato Fries

Serves: 3

Preparation Time: 10 minutes

Cooking Time: 25 minutes

Ingredients:

1 large sweet potato, peeled and cut into wedges

1 teaspoon ground turmeric

1 teaspoon ground cinnamon

Salt and freshly ground black pepper, to taste

1 tablespoon olive oil

Instructions:

Preheat the oven to 425 degrees F. Line a baking sheet with a piece of foil.

In a large bowl, add all ingredients and toss to coat well.

Transfer the mixture onto the prepared baking sheet in a single layer.

Bake for about 25 minutes, flipping once after 15 minutes.

Nutrition Information per Serving:

Calories: 79

Fat: 37.3g

Carbohydrates: 8g

Protein: 0

28. Kale Chips

Serves: 6

Preparation Time: 10 minutes

Cooking Time: 15 minutes

Ingredients:

1 pound fresh kale leaves, stemmed and torn

¼ teaspoon cayenne pepper

Salt, to taste

1 tablespoon olive oil

Instructions:

Preheat the oven to 350 degrees F. Line a large baking sheet with a parchment paper.

Place kale pieces onto the prepared baking sheet in a single layer.

Sprinkle the kale with salt and drizzle with oil.

Bake for about 10-15 minutes.

Nutrition Information per Serving:

Calories: 57

Fat: 2.3g

Carbohydrates: 8g

Protein: 2.3g

29. Zucchini Sticks

Serves: 8

Preparation Time: 10 minutes

Cooking Time: 25 minutes

Ingredients:

2 zucchinis, cut into 3-inch sticks lengthwise

Salt, to taste

2 organic eggs

½ cup Parmesan cheese, grated

½ cup almonds, grounded

½ teaspoon Italian herb seasoning

Instructions:

In a large colander, place zucchini sticks and sprinkle with salt.

Keep aside for about 1 hour to drain.

Preheat the oven to 425 degrees F. Line a large baking sheet with parchment paper.

Squeeze the zucchini sticks to remove excess liquid.

With a paper towel, pat dries the zucchini sticks.

In a shallow dish, crack the eggs and beat.

In another shallow dish, mix together remaining ingredients.

Dip the zucchini sticks in egg and then coat with the cheese mixture evenly.

Arrange the zucchini sticks into a prepared baking sheet in a single layer.

Bake for about 25 minutes, turning once halfway through.

Nutritional Information per Serving:

Calories: 133

Fat: 9.2g

Carbohydrates: 4.5g

Protein: 9.4g

30. Strawberry Gazpacho

Serves: 4

Preparation Time: 15 minutes

Ingredients:

3 large avocados, peeled, pitted and chopped

1/3 cup fresh cilantro leaves

3 cups homemade vegetable broth

2 tablespoons fresh lemon juice

1 teaspoon ground cumin

¼ teaspoon cayenne pepper

Salt, to taste

Instructions:

In a blender, add all ingredients and pulse until smooth.

Transfer the gazpacho into a large bowl.

Cover and refrigerate to chill completely before serving.

Nutrition Information per Serving:

Calories: 227

Fat: 20.4g

Carbohydrates: 9g

Protein: 4.5g

Camping Recipes

31. Nuts Granola

Serves: 10

Preparation Time: 15 minutes

Cooking Time: 18 minutes

Ingredients:

1½ cups almonds

1½ cups hazelnuts

¼ cup cacao powder

1 cup flax seeds meal

Pinch of sea salt

¼ cup hazelnut oil

¼ cup almond butter, melted

2-ounce unsweetened dark chocolate, chopped

1/3 cup erythritol

20 drops stevia extract

Instructions:

Preheat the oven to 300 degrees F. Line a large baking sheet with parchment paper.

In a food processor, add almonds and hazelnuts and pulse until coarse crumb forms.

Transfer the nut mixture into a large bowl.

Add cacao powder, flax seeds meal, and salt and mix well.

In a pan, add hazelnut oil, butter, and chocolate over low heat and cook for about 2-3 minutes or until smooth, stirring continuously.

Stir in swerve and immediately, remove from heat.

Add butter mixture over nut mixture and toss to coat well.

Transfer the mixture onto prepared baking sheet evenly.

Bake for about 15 minutes, stirring after every 5 minutes.

Turn off the oven but keep the baking sheet in oven for about 20 minutes, stirring occasionally.

Remove from oven and keep aside to cool completely.

This granola can be served with cream, non-daily milk, and fruit of your choice.

Nutrition Information per Serving:

Calories: 280

Fat: 23.1g

Carbohydrates: 8.1g

Protein: 9.2g

32. Zucchini Pancakes

Serves: 4

Preparation Time: 15 minutes

Cooking Time: 20 minutes

Ingredients:

1/3 cup water

2 tablespoons ground flax seeds

1 teaspoon coconut oil

3 large zucchinis, grated

Salt and freshly ground black pepper, to taste

¼ cup scallion, chopped finely

Instructions:

In a bowl, mix together flax seeds and water and keep aside.

In a large skillet, heat oil over medium heat and cook zucchini for about 2-3 minutes, stirring occasionally.

Stir in salt and black pepper and immediately, remove from heat.

Transfer the zucchini into a large bowl and keep aside to cool slightly.

Add flax seed mixture and scallion and mix until well combined.

Heat a greased nonstick skillet over medium heat.

Add ¼ of the zucchini mixture and cook for about 2-3 minutes.

Carefully flip the side and cook for 1-2 minutes more.

Repeat with the remaining mixture.

Serve warm.

Nutrition Information per Serving:

Calories: 69

Fat: 2.7g

Carbohydrates: 9g

Protein: 3.7g

33. Jasmine Green Tea

Serves: 2

Preparation Time: 10 minutes

Ingredients:

2½ cups boiling water

2 tablespoons loose leaf jasmine green tea

4 lemon slices

3-4 drops liquid stevia

Instructions:

In a pitcher, mix together all ingredients.

Cover and steep for about 3-5 minutes.

Serve immediately.

Nutrition Information per Serving:

Calories: 1

Fat: 0g

Carbohydrates: 0.4g

Protein: 0.1g

34. Mushroom Soup

Serves: 4

Preparation Time: 15 minutes

Cooking Time: 20 minutes

Ingredients:

2 teaspoons olive oil

1 small yellow onion, chopped

2 celery stalks, chopped

1 large carrot, peeled and chopped

2 garlic cloves, minced

Salt and freshly ground black pepper, to taste

6 cups vegetable broth

8-ounces fresh button mushrooms, sliced thinly

2 scallions, chopped

Instructions:

In a large pan, heat oil over medium heat and sauté onion, celery, carrot, and garlic for about 4-5 minutes.

Add broth and bring to a boil.

Cook for about 1-2 minutes.

Add mushrooms and bring to a boil.

Cook for about 6-7 minutes.

Stir in scallion and cook for about 2 minutes.

Serve hot.

Nutrition Information per Serving:

Calories: 110

Fat: 4.6g

Carbohydrates: 8g

Protein: 9.7g

35. Mixed Veggie Kabobs

Serves: 4

Preparation Time: 20 minutes

Cooking Time: 10 minutes

Ingredients:

For Marinade:

2 garlic cloves, minced

1 teaspoon fresh lemon peel, grated finely

1 teaspoon fresh rosemary, minced

1 teaspoon fresh basil, minced

2 tablespoons olive oil

2 tablespoons fresh lemon juice

Salt and freshly ground black pepper, to taste

For Veggies:

1 large zucchini, cut into thick slices

½ head of cauliflower, cut into florets

4 large button mushrooms, quartered

1 small yellow bell pepper, seeded and cut into large cubes

1 small red bell pepper, seeded and cut into large cubes

1 medium red onion, cut into large cubes

Instructions:

For marinade in a large bowl, add all ingredients and beat until well combined.

Add vegetables and toss to coat well.

Cover and refrigerate to marinate for at least 8-10 hours.

Preheat the grill to medium-high heat. Grease the grill grate.

Remove vegetables from the bowl and discard any excess marinade.

Thread the vegetables onto pre-soaked wooden skewers.

Grill for about 8-10 minutes or until desired doneness, flipping occasionally.

Serve warm.

Nutrition Information per Serving:

Calories: 122

Fat: 7.6g

Carbohydrates: 13g

Protein: 3.5g

36. Grilled Mushrooms

Serves: 3

Preparation Time: 15 minutes

Cooking Time: 14 minutes

Ingredients:

12- ounces fresh portabella mushrooms, stalks removed

¼ cup olive oil

2 teaspoons fresh lemon juice

1 teaspoon garlic, minced finely

Salt, to taste

1 tablespoon fresh parsley, chopped

Instructions:

Preheat the grill to high heat. grease the grill grate.

In a bowl, add oil, lemon juice, garlic, and salt and beat until well combined.

Coat the mushrooms with oil mixture generously.

Grill the mushrooms for about 5-7 minutes per side or until desired doneness.

Garnish with parsley and serve.

Nutrition Information per Serving:

Calories: 176

Fat: 17.1g

Carbohydrates: 6.2g

Protein: 2.9g

37. Curried Broccoli

Serves: 4

Preparation Time: 15 minutes

Cooking Time: 10 minutes

Ingredients:

¼ cup unsweetened coconut flakes

1 tablespoon coconut oil

½ of a small yellow onion sliced thinly

1 tablespoon fresh ginger, minced

2 teaspoons curry powder

1 teaspoon cumin seeds

Salt, to taste

2 tablespoons filtered water

1 pound fresh broccoli florets

Instructions:

Heat a large nonstick skillet over medium heat and cook coconut flakes for about 3-4 minutes, stirring continuously.

Transfer the toasted coconut flakes into a bowl and keep aside.

In the same skillet, heat oil over medium heat.

Add onion and sauté for about 3-4 minutes.

Add ginger and spices and sauté for about 1-2 minutes.

Add water and broccoli and stir to combine.

Increase the heat to medium-high and cook, covered for about 3-4 minutes.

Serve hot with the topping of toasted coconut flakes.

Nutrition Information per Serving:

Calories: 99

Fat: 5.6g

Carbohydrates: 11.1g

Protein: 3.9g

38. Mushroom with Green Beans

Serves: 2

Preparation Time: 15 minutes

Cooking Time: 18 minutes

Ingredients:

2 tablespoons butter

2 tablespoons yellow onion, minced

½ teaspoon garlic, minced

1 (8-ounce) package white mushrooms, sliced

1 cup frozen green beans

Salt and freshly ground black pepper, to taste

Instructions:

In a large skillet, melt butter over medium heat and sauté onion and garlic for about 1 minute.

Add mushrooms and cook for about 6-7 minutes.

Stir in green beans and cook for about 5-10 minutes or until desired doneness.

Serve hot.

Nutritional Information per Serving:

Calories: 148

Fat: 11.8g

Carbohydrates: 8.9g

Protein: 4.8g

39. Crunchy Veggie Salad

Serves: 4 Preparation Time: 15 minutes

Ingredients:

For Salad:

2 cups carrots, peeled and shredded

1½ cups green cabbage, shredded

1½ cups red cabbage, shredded

1 cup cucumber, sliced

2 large scallions, chopped

¼ cup fresh parsley leaves, chopped

For Dressing:

2 tablespoons olive oil

2 tablespoons fresh lemon juice

1 teaspoon fresh lemon zest, grated finely

Salt and freshly ground black pepper, to taste

Instructions:

For the salad: in a large serving bowl, add all ingredients and mix.

For dressing: in another bowl, all ingredients and beat until well combined.

Pour dressing over salad and toss to coat well.

Serve immediately.

Nutrition Information per Serving:

Calories: 107

Fat: 7.2g

Carbohydrates: 10.8g Protein: 1.7g

40. Cucumber Salad

Serves: 8

Preparation Time: 15 minutes

Ingredients:

For Dressing:

5 tablespoons olive oil

2 tablespoons fresh lemon juice

2 tablespoons fresh mint leaves, chopped finely

1 teaspoon Erythritol

Salt and freshly ground black pepper, to taste

For Salad:

2 cups cucumbers, peeled, seeded and sliced

10 cups fresh baby spinach

¼ of a medium red onion, sliced

Instructions:

For dressing: in another bowl, all ingredients and beat until well combined.

For the salad: in a large serving bowl, add all ingredients

Pour dressing over salad and toss to coat well.

Serve immediately.

Nutrition Information per Serving:

Calories: 96

Fat: 9.1g

Carbohydrates: 3.9g

Protein: 1.8g

Dessert Recipe

41. Cream Cheese Cookies

Serves: 24

Preparation Time: 15 minutes

Cooking Time: 15 minutes

Ingredients:

3 cups almond flour

¼ teaspoon salt

½ cup Erythritol

2-ounce cream cheese softened

¼ cup butter softened

1 large organic egg white

2 teaspoons organic vanilla extract

Instructions:

Preheat the oven to 350 degrees F. Line a larger cookie sheet with baking paper.

In a bowl, add flour and salt and mix well. Set aside.

Add Erythritol, cream cheese and butter in the bowl of stand mixer and mix until fluffy and light.

Now, place the egg white and vanilla extract and mix until well combined.

Slowly, add flour mixture, ½ cup at a time and beat until a little crumbly dough is formed.

With a medium cookie scooper, place the mixture onto the prepared baking sheet about 1-inch apart and with your hand, flatten each ball slightly.

Bake for about 15 minutes.

Remove from oven and place the cookie sheet onto a wire rack to cool completely before serving.

Nutritional Information per Serving:

Calories: 111

Fat: 9.4g

Carbohydrates: 3.1g

Protein: 3.4g

42. Zucchini Brownies

Serves: 16

Preparation Time: 15 minutes

Cooking Time: 25 minutes

Ingredients:

1¼ cups 70% dark chocolate chips

1/3 cup coconut oil

¾ cup granulated Erythritol

¼ cup zucchini, shredded finely and squeezed

2 large organic eggs

3 tablespoons arrowroot powder

2 tablespoons cacao powder

Instructions:

Preheat the oven to 350 degrees F. Line an 8x8-inch baking dish with a lightly greased piece of foil.

In a microwave-safe bowl, add chocolate chips and coconut oil and microwave until melted and smooth.

Remove from the microwave and transfer the mixture into a large bowl.

Add zucchini, Erythritol, and eggs and beat until well combined.

Add arrowroot powder and cacao powder and beat until smooth.

In the prepared baking dish, place the mixture evenly and with a spatula, smooth the top surface.

Bake for about 20-25 minutes.

Remove from oven and place the baking dish onto a wire rack to cool completely.

After cooling, cut into desired size squares and serve.

Nutritional Information per Serving:

Calories: 100

Fat: 7.8g

Carbohydrates: 8.2g

Protein: 1.6g

43. Peanut Butter Fudge

Serves: 16

Preparation Time: 15 minutes

Cooking Time: 5 minutes

Ingredients:

1½ cups creamy, salted peanut butter

1/3 cup butter

2/3 cup powdered Erythritol

¼ cup unsweetened protein powder

1 teaspoon organic vanilla extract

Instructions:

In a small pan, add peanut butter and butter over low heat and cook until melted and smooth.

Add Erythritol and protein powder and mix until smooth.

Remove from heat and stir in vanilla extract.

Place the fudge mixture into a baking paper lined 8x8-inch baking dish evenly and with a spatula, smooth the top surface.

Freeze for about 30-45 minutes or until set completely.

Carefully, transfer the fudge onto a cutting board with the help of the parchment paper.

Cut the fudge into equal sized squares and serve.

Nutritional Information per Serving:

Calories: 183

Fat: 16.1g

Carbohydrates: 4.8g

Protein: 7.4g

44. Cinnamon Donuts

Serves: 16

Preparation Time: 15 minutes

Cooking Time: 28 minutes

Ingredients:

For Donuts:

1 cup almond flour

1/3 cup Erythritol

2 teaspoons organic baking powder

1 teaspoon ground cinnamon

1/8 teaspoon salt

2 large organic eggs

¼ cup unsweetened almond milk

¼ cup unsalted butter (measured solid, then melted)

½ teaspoon organic vanilla extract

For Coating:

½ cup Erythritol

1 teaspoon ground cinnamon

3 tablespoons unsalted butter (measured solid, then melted)

Instructions:

Preheat the oven to 350 degrees F. Generously, grease a donut pan.

For donut: in a large bowl, add almond flour, Erythritol, baking powder, cinnamon, and salt and mix well.

In another bowl, add eggs, almond milk, butter, and vanilla extract and beat until well combined.

Add the egg mixture into flour mixture and mix until well combined.

Transfer the mixture into prepared donut holes about ¾ of the way full.

Bake for about 22-28 minutes.

Remove from oven and put the donut pa onto a wire rack to cool slightly before removing from the pan.

Meanwhile, for coating: in a small bowl, add Erythritol and cinnamon and mix well.

Carefully, remove the donuts from pan and transfer onto a cutting board.

Coat the donuts with melted butter evenly and then, roll in the cinnamon mixture before serving.

Nutritional Information per Serving:

Calories: 261

Fat: 24.1g

Carbohydrates: 5.7g

Protein: 6.3g

45. Cream Cake

Serves: 12

Preparation Time: 15 minutes

Cooking Time: 50 minutes

Ingredients:

2 cups almond flour

2 teaspoons organic baking powder

½ cup butter, chopped

2-ounces cream cheese softened

1 cup sour cream

1 cup Erythritol

1 teaspoon organic vanilla extract

4 large organic eggs

Instructions:

Preheat the oven to 350 degrees F. Generously, grease a 9-inch Bundt pan.

In a large bowl, add almond flour and baking powder and mix well. Set aside.

In a microwave-safe bowl, add butter and cream cheese and microwave for about 30 seconds.

Remove from microwave and stir well.

Add sour cream, Erythritol and vanilla extract and mix until well combined.

Add the cream mixture into the bowl of flour mixture and mix until well combined.

Add eggs and mix until well combined.

Transfer the mixture into the prepared pan evenly.

Bake for about 50 minutes or until a toothpick inserted in the center comes out clean.

Remove from oven and put onto a wire rack to cool completely before removing the pan.

Carefully, invert the cake from the pan.

Cut into desired sized slices and serve.

Nutritional Information per Serving:

Calories: 263

Fat: 23.9g

Carbohydrates: 5.5g

Protein: 7.2g

46. Simple Cheesecake

Serves: 16

Preparation Time: 20 minutes

Cooking Time: 1 hour 7 minutes

Ingredients:

For Crust:

2 cups almond flour

1/3 cup butter, melted

3 tablespoons Erythritol

1 teaspoon organic vanilla extract

For Filling:

32-ounce cream cheese softened

1¼ cups powdered Erythritol

3 large organic eggs

1 tablespoon fresh lemon juice

1 teaspoon organic vanilla extract

Instructions:

Preheat the oven to 350 degrees F. Line a 9-inch greased springform with a piece of foil.

For crust: in a bowl, add all ingredients and mix until a crumbly mixture is formed.

Place the crust into prepared pan, pressing in the bottom and a little up the sides.

Bake for about 10-12 minutes.

Remove from the oven and set aside onto a wire rack to cool for at least 10 minutes.

For filling: in a large bowl, add the cream cheese and Erythritol and beat until fluffy.

Add eggs, 1 at a time and with a wire whisk, beat until well combined after each addition.

Add the lemon juice and vanilla extract and beat until well combined.

Place the filling over the crust evenly and with the back of a spatula, smooth the top surface.

Bake for about 45-55 minutes.

Remove from the oven and set aside onto a wire rack to cool completely.

Refrigerate for about 4 hours.

Cut into desired sized slices and serve.

Nutritional Information per Serving:

Calories: 331

Fat: 31.2g

Carbohydrates: 4.7g

Protein: 8.5g

47. Blueberry Cobbler

Serves: 10

Preparation Time: 15 minutes

Cooking Time: 22 minutes

Ingredients:

For Filling:

3 cups fresh blueberries

2 tablespoons Erythritol

¼ teaspoon xanthan gum

1 teaspoon fresh lemon juice

For Topping:

2/3 cup almond flour

2 tablespoons Erythritol

2 tablespoons butter, melted

½ teaspoon fresh lemon zest, grated finely

Instructions:

Preheat the oven to 375 degrees F.

For filling: in a bowl, add all ingredients and mix well.

Transfer the mixture into a 9-inch baking dish and with the back of the spoon, press to smooth the surface.

For topping: in a bowl, add all ingredients and mix until a crumbly mixture forms.

Place the crumble mixture over blueberry mixture evenly.

Bake for about 22 minutes or until top becomes golden brown.

Serve warm.

Nutritional Information per Serving:

Calories: 88

Fat: 6.2g

Carbohydrates: 8g

Protein: 2g

48. Vanilla Flan

Serves: 6

Preparation Time: 15 minutes

Cooking Time: 1 hour 10 minutes

Ingredients:

1 cup Erythritol, divided

1 cup plus 1 tablespoon water, divided

5 organic eggs

1/8 teaspoon salt

1¾ cups heavy cream

1 teaspoon organic vanilla extract

Instructions:

Preheat the oven to 325 degrees F.

For caramel: in a small pan, add ½ cup of Erythritol and 1 tablespoon of water over medium-low heat and cook until sweetener is melted completely, stirring continuously.

Remove from the heat and place the caramel in the bottom of a round baking dish evenly.

Set aside for about 10 minutes.

In a bowl, add the remaining Erythritol, eggs, and salt and beat until well combined. Set aside.

In a medium pan, add remaining water and cream and bring to a boil.

Remove from the heat.

Slowly, add hot cream mixture into egg yolk mixture, beating continuously until well combined.

Add the mixture into the pan with the remaining cream mixture and mix well.

Now, place the vanilla extract and mix well.

Place the cream mixture over the caramel in the baking dish evenly.

Arrange the baking dish in a large roasting pan.

Add hot water in the roasting pan about 1-inch up sides of the baking dish.

Place the roasting pan in oven and bake for about 55-60 minutes or until center becomes set.

Remove from oven and place the baking dish onto a wire rack to cool for about 1 hour.

Refrigerate to chill completely before serving.

Nutritional Information per Serving:

Calories: 175

Fat: 16.6g

Carbohydrates: 1.4g

Protein: 5.3g

49. Chocolate Mousse

Serves: 2

Preparation Time: 10 minutes

Ingredients:

2½ cups water, divided

1 cup ricotta cheese

2 teaspoons powdered stevia

2 teaspoons cacao powder

½ teaspoon organic vanilla extract

Instructions:

In a large bowl, place all the ingredients and beat until well combined.

Transfer the mousse into 2 serving glasses and refrigerate to chill for about 4-6 hours or until set completely.

Serve chilled.

Nutritional Information per Serving:

Calories: 178

Fat: 10.1g

Carbohydrates: 7.3g

Protein: 14.5g

50. Raspberry Mousse

Serves: 4

Preparation Time: 15 minutes

Ingredients:

2½ cups fresh raspberries

1/3 cup Erythritol

1/3 cup unsweetened almond milk

1 tablespoon fresh lemon juice

1 teaspoon liquid stevia

¼ teaspoon salt

Instructions:

In a food processor, put all ingredients and pulse until smooth.

Transfer into an ice cream maker and process according to manufacturer's directions.

Now, place into an airtight container and freeze for at least 4-5 hours before serving.

Nutritional Information per Serving:

Calories: 44

Fat: 0.8g

Carbohydrates: 9.4g

Protein: 1g

Chapter Five:
Frequently Asked Questions

There are many general questions regarding the keto diet and most of them have been tried to answer in the above-written introductions. Yet, a few frequently asked questions along with their answers regarding keto diets are given below:

How much weight loss will I experience on a keto diet?

The result for weight loss varies from person to person on a wider scale. Mostly in the initial stages usually people lose around 2-4 lbs. i.e. 1-2kgs in the first week, this particular weight loss is related to water weight. Afterward, generally, people do lose approximately 1 lb. or half a kilogram of fat every week. However, this rate may vary and certain people might experience a faster rate of weight loss (mostly younger males) and some people might experience slower weight loss rate (usual women above 40).

As soon as you reach your normal body weight, the process of weight loss will become slower. As long as you keep on consuming food when you are hungry, your weight will get stabilized despite being on a ketogenic diet plan.

How do I keep a track of my carb consumption?

In most cases, the diet is devised in a manner which will keep your carb consumption below 20 net carbs/day, without the urge to count it at all. If it is not mentioned in the diet plan, there are certain ways by which carb intake can be calculated. These include the most widely used methods like using apps i.e. Chronometer or MyFitnessPal.

What happens after I achieve my health and weight aims on keto?

As you accomplish achieving your goals on the keto plan, you can either opt for carrying on with the keto plan to maintain the effects or on the other hand, you can add some additional carbs to your diet plan. In case you add a bit of carb to your plan, there is a possibility that the effectiveness of the keto plan will be lowered and it might or might not result in gaining some weight.

If you opt for completely unfollow the keto plan, with a gradual passage of time you will experience the very same conditions and symptoms as you had before prior to the following of the keto plan. It is just like exercising on daily basis, once you stop, you stop gaining the benefits. Keto diet plans are effective until you are following them.

Is optimal Ketosis Important for Experience the Benefits?

No, most of the benefits i.e. weight loss etc. can be experienced at much lower ketosis levels i.e. above 0.5 mmol/l. But, the higher levels of ketosis are important for having better physical and mental performances. The body takes a certain time limit to get used to the ketosis and adapt it completely.

What should be the total carb intake on Keto?

It is important to know that in order to be in ketosis the carbs/100g should be lower. For achieving ketosis, it is essential to avoid consuming carbs in higher quantity. The carbs intake should be no more than 50g/day of total carbs, for efficient working, it should be approximately below 20g/day. The idea is that the lesser the carbs intake, the more efficient will the diet plan work.

What are the potential side effects of the keto vegetarian diet?

With the sudden shift of your metabolism towards fats and ketone burning from burning carbs or glucose, there come certain side effects on your body as the body is adapting the new energy source being supplied to it. These side effects may have the symptoms of tiredness, headache, cramping, heart palpitations, and muscle fatigue. These symptoms are generally experienced for a very short time span and fade away as the body gets adjusted with ketosis. Most people don't experience them, and even in case if you encounter these symptoms, they can be reduced or cured in different ways.

To lower the possible side effects of keto diet on you, you can opt for gradually lowering your carb consumption rather than stopping its intake at once. This comes with a drawback that the slower starting rate will not result in drastic changes in your body and the plan will not be as effective as compared to the immediate halting of carb intake.

Hence, it is preferred to halt the intake of starch and sugar all at once. This will result in weight loss of many pounds in just a few days. Though the initial weight loss is only due to a reduction in swelling, this will motivate you to follow the plan more effectively and will certainly result in drastic changes in your body.

Keto Flu

As you start following the keto plan, almost every individual experience the following symptoms for a couple of days. These symptoms are generally referred to as having 'keto flu'. The symptoms are stated as below:

- A headache.

- Dizziness.

- Fatigue.

- Light nausea.

- Lack of motivation.

- Difficulty focusing also called 'brain fog'.

- Irritability.

If you experience these symptoms, you don't have to worry as they fade away in the initial week of following the plan as the body gets itself normalized to fat burning instead of carbs. The main reason for keto flu is that foods having a higher amount of carbs result in a phenomenon known as water retention or swelling in the body. With the consumption of a low carb diet, a larger amount of this fluid vanishes which will result in frequent urination alongside the loss of a certain amount of extra salt too. This results in dehydration of the body and the lack of salt prior to the adaption of ketosis by your body. This is credit as the main factor for the symptoms of keto flu. These symptoms can be lowered or even eliminated simply by ensuring enough intakes of water and salt.

What are the general side effects of the keto vegetarian diet?

There are five more side effects of the keto diet apart from the keto flu. The remedy to avoid these symptoms is also ensuring the proper and enough intakes of water and salts alongside having proper treatment for these specific issues:

- Constipation

- Leg Cramps

- Keto Breath

- Reduced Physical Performance

- Heart Palpitations

What are the rare side effects of the keto vegetarian diet?

Apart from the general and common side effects, there are a few rare side effects of keto diet which are experienced very rarely by a comparatively lower group of individuals and there are certain measures to deal with them. These symptoms are as follows:

- Gallstone Complications.

- Gout.

- Elevated Cholesterol Levels.

- Temporary Hair Loss.

- Reduced Tolerance to Alcohol.

- Potential Dangers while Breastfeeding.

- Keto Rash.

What are the myths related to the keto diet?

Generally, most of the side effects experienced by keto followers in the start are for a very short time span and are temporary in nature. But, there are certain myths regarding keto which does scare off people. These include vague ideas like your brain will halt to function in the absence of higher carb intake. This is a myth which is created by failing to understand the entire process of ketosis and how fats are used as an energy source instead of carbs or glucose.

One more general mistake is jumbling up normal ketosis process which is a result of the ketogenic diet with the fatal medical complication known as ketoacidosis. These two phenomena are certainly different and the latter doesn't occur due to following a keto diet plan at all.

What are the symptoms of Ketosis?

There are many ways to know that you are in ketosis which includes a breath or blood sample, urine testing. In addition to these tests, there are physical symptoms of ketosis which don't require any test at all. They are as follows:

Increase Thirst & Dry Mouth

There is a possibility of having a dry mouth if you aren't consuming enough electrolytes like salt etc. or drink enough water. It is recommended to drink as much water as possible alongside consuming enough bouillon i.e. 1-2 cups daily. There will be a certain metallic taste in your body.

Increase in Urination

A ketonic compound called 'acetoacetate' might end up in urine. This makes it easy to test ketosis via using urine strips. In the initial stages, it also results in frequent urination. It is the main reason for the increase in thirst (explained above).

Keto breath

The specific breath called the 'keto breath' is due to a compound called acetone, escaping via the breath. It results in making the breath having a certain 'fruity' smell or a smell similar to that of nail paint remover. You can also sense this certain smell after sweating while doing a workout in the gym. This condition is temporary and fades away with time.

Other signs which are positive in nature are as follows:

Increase in Energy

After passing through the 'keto flu', which results in tiredness, people experience a certain increase in energy levels. It can also be experienced in the form increased focus and concentration or even in the sense of having a euphoria.

Reduction in Hunger

This can be credited to the body utilizing the surplus energy from the stored fats. People feel satisfied with only one or two diets a day resulting in intermittent fasting unconsciously, saving both money and time alongside speeding the weight loss factor.

Chapter Six:
Common Mistakes by Beginners

The keto diet can be very confusing to beginners and they might unintentionally be committing mistakes which are going to hinder the effectiveness of the diet plan. Some of them are as follows:

Obsession with Weight Scale

Everyone's body reacts differently to the keto diet; some may lose weight instantly while others might take some time in achieving weight loss. Above all the keto diet isn't only about weight so don't have the obsession of merely the weight scale.

Taking Processed Fats

Seed and vegetable oils are mostly processed fats and are a health danger. They cause conditions like cancer, increasing cholesterol levels, and even heart attacks.

Not consuming Adequate Fats

It is very hard to maintain your fat intake while being new to keto. Maintain a proper intake of fats to make the plan work.

Avoiding Meal Planning

Meal planning is very necessary for keto diet. If you don't plan, you will eventually lose access to the required macros and end up eating food which might knock you out of your ketosis. Plan effectively to follow the keto diet.

Excessive Protein Intake

Proteins in keto are used to maintaining the main muscle mass and fats are used as the energy source only. Excessive protein intake can result in increasing glucose levels which will affect your ketosis. Planning your diet can maintain your protein intake as required.

Keto Isn't a Quick Fix

Keto isn't just a diet, it's a complete lifestyle. Following it for a short time and then leaving the plan will lead you to exactly where you started it. If you are looking for a quick fix for your weight, simply cut off sugar from your diet, but keto is a lifetime thing, adapt it.

Stop Comparing

Keto might react differently to different people. Everyone has a different body effect to the diet, stop comparing yourself to the result of other. Instead, focus on following your diet strictly to achieve your results and lice a healthy lifestyle.

Stay Hydrated

Drinking an effective water intake is very necessary for keto followers. You might be losing water in sweating, drink enough to remain hydrated

Conclusion

The ketogenic diet plan is based on the process of ketosis. The process of ketosis involves changing the metabolism of the body from utilizing carbs or glucose as an energy source to fat burning or ketones. The process of ketosis is achieved with the gradual passage of time and has been credited with different stages based on the variation in the ketone levels. The ketogenic diet plan has many benefits including weight loss, high physical and mental performances, treatment and reversal of type 2 diabetes, treatment of cancer, epilepsy, treatment of Alzheimer's disease and even Parkinson's disease.

With all these benefits, it also has certain side effects which are mostly temporary in nature and can be easily avoided or reduced. The symptoms of ketosis fade away as soon as the body gets adjusted with ketosis. The ketogenic vegetarian plan is effective for everybody and the weight loss rate might vary from person to person. The plan is very effective and once you stop following it, you may experience the same symptoms as before the adaption of the plan. The plan is not very expensive and there are certain methods and meals which make the plan not a burden on your budget.

-- Emily Lewis --

Made in the USA
Middletown, DE
03 May 2019